The Fearsome Four

Written by Susan Griffiths

Illustrated by Chris Lynch

Contents   Page

Chapter 1.   4
A bully at school

Chapter 2.   8
Safety in numbers

Chapter 3.   14
A plan to get Sid

Chapter 4.   18
Bully lessons

Chapter 5.   26
A serious problem

Verse   32

Rigby

The Fearsome Four

With these characters ...

Sid Fitzpatrick

Harley Scott

David Scott

Natasha di Carlo

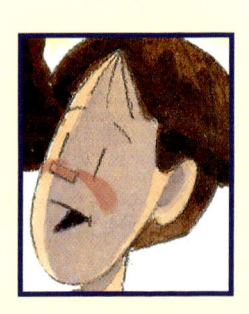

Sam Markovic

"He had a

Setting the scene ...

Sid Fitzpatrick is the school bully. But four students decide that he has been a bully for long enough. They become the Fearsome Four.

Sid soon learns what it feels like to be bullied — but will the Fearsome Four go too far?

mean-looking smile ..."

Chapter 1.

Harley Scott shouted and squirmed, but it was no use. Sid Fitzpatrick was trying to shove him into an empty locker. Sid was much bigger and stronger than Harley.

Harley shouted and squirmed.
He didn't want Sid to lock him in his locker.

Just then, his twin brother, David, walked down the hall and saw Harley squeezed into his locker.

"Hey, Harley. What happened this time?" David asked.

Harley screwed up his face. "That . . . bully, Sid caught me again," he said. "Help me get out, will you?"

"Ouch!" said David. "You're stuck in a tight spot!"

"Phew!" said Harley, after he was set free. "That locker wasn't very big!" He then slammed the locker door shut.

Chapter 2.

Before school the next morning, Harley and David told their friends, Natasha and Sam, what Sid had done.
Just then, Sid Fitzpatrick walked past. He had a mean-looking smile on his face.

"I want to teach Sid a lesson about bullying," whispered Harley to the others. Natasha was interested, because Sid had pulled her glasses off last week.

"Safety in numbers!" said Sam, munching on a banana. "My dad says there's safety in numbers."

"What does that mean?" asked David.

"If we stick together, Sid won't be able to bully us. He can bully one of us — but he can't bully four of us at the same time," said Sam.

"That's right!" said Harley. "From now on, we will go everywhere and do everything *together*."

No longer would they be the fearful four. They were about to become the Fearsome Four! Watch out, Sid!

That night, Harley and David worked out three secret plans to teach Harley a lesson. They also designed Fearsome Four membership cards on the computer.

The next morning, Harley and David arrived at school early. They waited in the hall for the others to arrive. Inside folders, they had their secret plans and membership cards for Natasha and Sam.

Behind them, they heard footsteps. They turned around. In an instant, they were staring into the face of their enemy, Sid Fitzpatrick.

"This time, I'm going to put both of you in a locker! Then I will close the door!" he snarled.

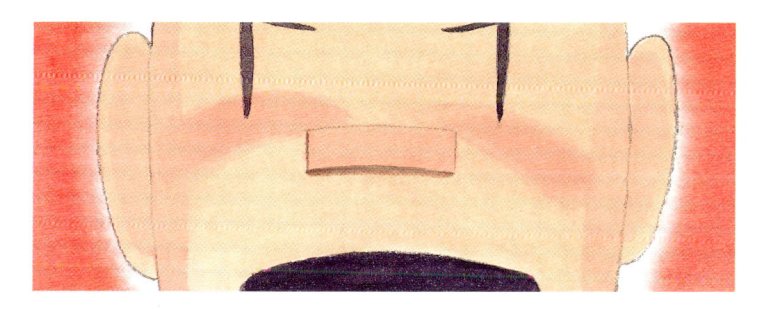

"No . . . please, no . . .," pleaded Harley. But it was no use. Sid grabbed him.

"STOP!" came a voice. Each of them jumped as they looked around.
Two shadows appeared in the doorway.

Chapter 3.

Sid recognized the shadows. "Come and watch your nerdy friends get squeezed into a locker," he snickered. He wasn't afraid of Natasha or Sam.

"No," said Natasha. "We're on duty in the nurse's office."

"And, *you're* going to feel sick all day!" said Sam.

The Fearsome Four surrounded Sid and pushed him into the nurse's office. Sid was so surprised he didn't know what to do. Natasha took the key from the door, slammed it shut, and locked it.

The Fearsome Four grinned at each other. "Just the right place for a sick person like Sid," said David.

The Fearsome Four were upset when a teacher rescued Sid from the nurse's office.

The next day, during lunchtime, they saw Sid from across the playground. He scowled at them and walked away.

"I didn't like the way Sid scowled at us," said Sam, shaking his head.

"Well he wasn't in that nurse's office for long enough to learn his lesson," David whispered.

"Let's teach that bully another lesson," said Natasha, chuckling.

The Fearsome Four huddled together and talked about their second secret plan.

Chapter 4.

That afternoon, after the bell rang, all the students collected their bags from their lockers. Sid pushed his way past the students. They quickly moved out of his way. Only the Fearsome Four stayed behind.

Sid tried to look calm and pushed himself against the door.

"What do you Foursome Losers want?" he asked rudely.

"Your shoelace is undone," said Harley, pointing down at Sid's shoe.

Sid looked down. In a second, the Fearsome Four were on top of him. Sid couldn't believe they tricked him.

Harley and David held Sid's arms.

Natasha and Sam grabbed a shoe each and tied the shoelaces together in tight, tricky knots. Sid couldn't walk.

"See you in the morning," said David.

Sid looked worried. He looked down at the knots in his shoelaces and wondered how he would ever be able to untie such a mess of knots.

"Next time you need help with your shoelaces, let us know," laughed Harley, as the Fearsome Four left the school.

Luckily for Sid, the custodian found him and helped him untie the knots in his laces.

The next day, Sid stayed well away from the Fearsome Four. At lunchtime, he stared at the grass as he ate his lunch.

The Fearsome Four spent their lunchtime planning their third bully lesson for Sid. After all the nasty things he had done to them, they thought it was only fair. Anyway, they liked the scared look on Sid's face.

Chapter 5.

The next morning, their teacher walked into the classroom with an angry look on her face.

"I have something serious to talk to you all about," she said, looking at the students. "We have a problem with bullies in our class."

Harley, David, Natasha, and Sam thought that Sid was going to get into big trouble again. The girl behind Sid kicked his chair. Sid stared down at his desk feeling sorry for himself. The Fearsome Four folded their arms, feeling good about themselves.

"Stand up when I read out your name. Today, we are going to stop this bullying," said the teacher sternly. She frowned at the students. Harley had a paper dart ready to throw at Sid when he stood up.

"Natasha di Carlo. Sam Markovic. David Scott. Harley Scott, *and* Sid Fitzpatrick," read the teacher.

They couldn't believe their ears. What was going on? Why did the teacher call their names first? Surely Sid was the only real bully in the class. Their knees felt like jelly as they slowly stood up.

"Go to the principal's office. NOW!" the teacher said sternly. She pointed at the door.

The Fearsome Four just became the Fearful Foursome.

The principal was very angry with their bullying. For the future, she reminded them to report any bullying to their teacher. Finally, the principal told them that she would call their parents! They felt embarrassed and ashamed. The principal then gave them punishments for bullying.

The next Monday after school, Sid and the Fearsome Four all worked as a team to empty the trash cans around the school.

On Tuesday, the team was on shoelace duty for the kindergarten children.

"Look at Sid!" said Harley to the others. "He's being really nice to the younger children and to the older students, too!"

On Wednesday afternoon, the Fearsome Four and Sid made "Good Behavior" posters to hang around the school. Sid's poster was the best. It showed a mean-looking student covered by a big red X. Underneath it said NO BULLIES in big red letters.

"Wow!" said Harley. "You're really good at drawing, Sid."

The next day before school started, Harley dropped his Fearsome Four membership card in a trash can. As it fluttered down, he saw three other membership cards at the bottom of the trash can.

Harley, David, Sam, Natasha *and* Sid had learned their lesson about bullying. For them, the problem no longer existed.

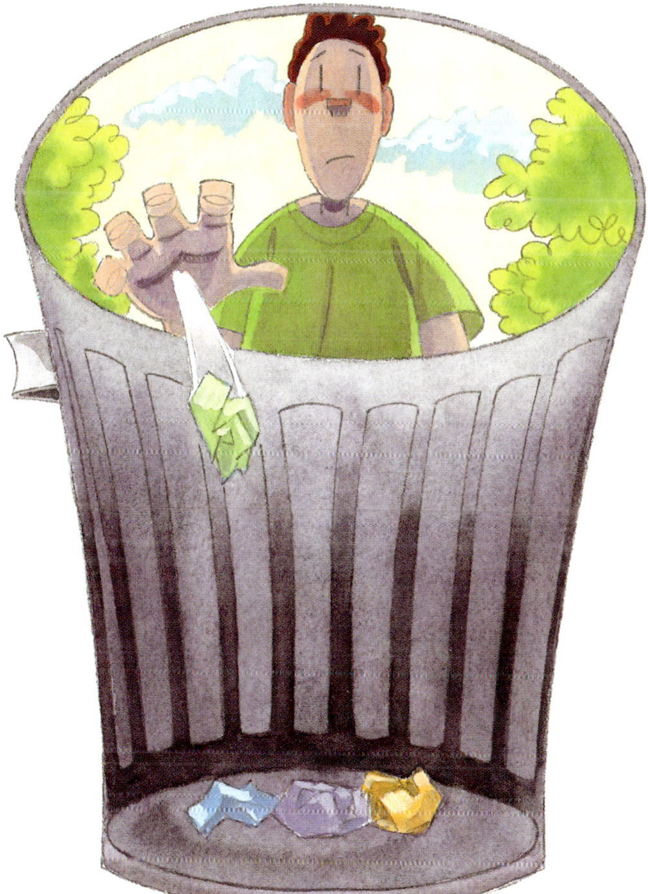

"When The Bully Is YOU!"

While there's safety in numbers
Be careful, you might
Be tempted to do things
That are wrong, not right.

It's not always easy
To face bullies, it's true;
It becomes even harder
When the bully is YOU!